I0408875

Save Till You Get Rich And Beyond

Dear Reader,

Welcome to "Save Till You Get Rich And Beyond," a guide to achieving financial success through the power of saving. In a world that often encourages us to spend beyond our means, this book aims to provide you with practical strategies and valuable insights to help you build wealth and secure your financial future.

In today's society, it's easy to fall into the trap of instant gratification and excessive spending. We are bombarded with messages that emphasize the importance of material possessions and the idea that happiness can be bought. However, true financial security and freedom come from adopting a different mindset—one that prioritizes saving and long-term financial goals.

"Save Till You Get Rich And Beyond" is not about deprivation or denying yourself the things you enjoy. Instead, it is a roadmap that encourages you to make conscious choices, prioritize your financial well-being, and make your money work for you. By embracing the power of saving, you can break free from the cycle of living paycheck to paycheck and create a future filled with abundance and opportunity.

Throughout this book, we will explore various topics, including:

The importance of setting financial goals: Learn how to define your financial aspirations and set achievable targets that align with your values and dreams.

Developing a budgeting system: Discover practical techniques for managing your income, tracking expenses, and maximizing savings potential.

Strategies for cutting expenses: Explore ways to trim unnecessary costs, reduce debt, and adopt a frugal mindset without sacrificing your quality of life.

Investing wisely: Gain insights into different investment options and learn how to make informed decisions to grow your wealth over time.

Building an emergency fund: Understand the significance of having a financial safety net and learn how to establish an emergency fund that can protect you during challenging times.

Overcoming common challenges: Address obstacles such as impulse buying, peer pressure, and societal expectations to stay on track with your saving goals.

Remember, financial success is not an overnight achievement. It requires discipline, perseverance, and a commitment to long-term planning. By implementing the principles and strategies outlined in this book, you can pave the way towards a future where financial freedom and abundance are within your reach.

So, join us on this journey towards financial empowerment. Let "Save Till You Get Rich And Beyond" be your guide as you take control of your finances and embark on a path towards a more prosperous and fulfilling life.

Happy saving!

Olusegun Akinola

For many people, setting and adhering to a saving plan appeared to be inconceivable. Though they would make a draft of the amount they needed to spend for the month ahead but yet wouldn't be able to stick to their plan after a few couple of days they started.

If you are like that, you need to change your attitude and treat saving with more seriousness.

You need to know that saving is not hard as most people think. Saving becomes easier if we have a plan.

In this book, I will show you how you can start saving like never before by creating a saving plan and budget that is reasonable, adaptable, and which could assist you with accomplishing your financial goals and obligations.

Keep on reading to know the savings and budget strategies that could make you save money till you get rich and beyond.

Before I proceed and for better understanding, let me differentiate between the three terms that I used frequently in this book; budget, saving and savings.

Budget is an estimate of your revenue and expected expenses for a given time period while savings refers to the money left over after your expenses are subtracted from your revenue, also within a specific time period. Savings refers to something that exists at any one time, a stock variable whereas saving refers to an activity occurring over time, a flow variable. Meaning money you have saved is called savings while saving is the act of saving money.

Budgeting is a vital process if one has any desire to save more and spend less. Budget provides people with a thought of the amount they are spending and the amount they can save.

Now, below are the savings and budget practices that can help you save money till you get rich and they will help you to skyrocket your financial worth.

Create a budget

In order to be able to save, you must have a deep interest in it and see it as important or necessary. Nobody can force someone else into saving, it is something we do ourselves out of our willingness.

Therefore, you will need to create a budget if you really want to save. Your budget should be in relevance to your income and include both daily expenses and occasional expenses. Start saving with an amount that will be convenient for you which will be subject to adjustment.

How creating a budget can make you save till you get rich and beyond

Creating a budget can be an effective tool for saving money because it helps you gain control over your finances and make intentional decisions about your spending. Here's how creating a budget can help you save:

Increased awareness: By creating a budget, you become more aware of your income, expenses, and spending patterns. You get a clear picture of where your money is going and can identify areas where you may be overspending or wasting money.

Setting financial goals: A budget allows you to set specific financial goals, such as saving for a down payment on a house, paying off debt, or building an emergency fund. When you have clear objectives, it becomes easier to allocate your income towards these goals, making saving a priority.

Prioritizing expenses: With a budget, you can allocate your money to cover essential expenses like housing, utilities, groceries, and debt payments before considering discretionary spending. By prioritizing your expenses, you ensure that your basic needs are met while being more mindful of unnecessary purchases.

Identifying areas for cost-cutting: Budgeting helps you identify areas where you can reduce expenses and save money. Analyzing your spending habits can reveal patterns of overspending or unnecessary expenditures, allowing you to make adjustments and find ways to cut costs. For example, you might discover that you spend too much on dining out or subscriptions that you don't use frequently.

Tracking progress: A budget helps you track your progress towards your savings goals. Regularly reviewing your budget allows you to see if you're staying on track, making adjustments as necessary, and celebrating milestones along the way. This tracking reinforces good financial habits and motivates you to continue saving.

Building an emergency fund: A budget enables you to allocate a portion of your income towards an emergency fund. Having an emergency fund provides a financial safety net and helps you avoid going into debt when unexpected expenses arise, such as medical bills or car repairs.

Planning for the future: Budgeting allows you to plan for future expenses, such as vacations, home improvements, or retirement. By saving a little each month in accordance with your budget, you can meet these goals without relying on credit or disrupting your overall financial stability.

Remember, creating a budget is just the first step. It's important to regularly review and adjust your budget as circumstances change. By sticking to your budget and consistently saving, you can develop healthier financial habits and achieve your long-term savings goals.

Avoiding impulsive purchases: When you have a budget in place, you're less likely to make impulsive purchases. By planning your expenses and having a clear understanding of what you can afford, you can avoid unnecessary spending on items that don't align with your priorities or financial goals.

Debt management: Budgeting can help you manage and reduce your debt. By allocating a portion of your income towards debt payments and prioritizing high-interest debts, you can make steady progress in paying off your loans. As you pay down your debts, you'll free up more money to put towards savings.

Saving on interest and fees: When you budget and make consistent payments on your bills and debts, you can avoid late fees, penalties, and high-interest charges. By being organized and staying on top of your financial obligations, you can save money that would otherwise be wasted on unnecessary fees or additional interest.

Negotiating better deals: With a budget, you can identify areas where you may be able to negotiate better deals or find more cost-effective alternatives. For example, you might negotiate lower insurance premiums, find cheaper utility providers, or shop around for better prices on essential items. These savings can add up significantly over time.

Building discipline and financial awareness: Budgeting requires discipline and a conscious effort to manage your money effectively. By practicing budgeting regularly, you develop financial awareness and become more mindful of your spending habits. This increased discipline can lead to smarter financial decisions and a greater ability to resist impulse purchases, ultimately helping you save more money.

Creating a buffer for unexpected expenses: Life is full of surprises, and having a budget allows you to prepare for unexpected expenses. By including a category for miscellaneous or emergency expenses in your budget, you can set aside some money each month to create a buffer for unexpected events. This helps prevent these unexpected costs from derailing your financial stability or forcing you into debt.

In summary, creating a budget empowers you to take control of your finances, prioritize your spending, and develop better saving habits. It provides a roadmap for your financial journey, enabling you to achieve your short-term and long-term savings goals while avoiding unnecessary expenses and fees.

Illustration:
Let's take a look at an illustration of how creating a budget can help you save:

Let's say your monthly income is $3,000, and you decide to create a budget to better manage your finances and save money. Here's a breakdown of your budget:

Fixed Expenses:

Rent: $1,000
Utilities (electricity, water, internet): $200
Insurance (car, health): $150
Debt payments (student loan, credit card): $300
Variable Expenses:

Groceries: $300
Transportation (fuel, public transportation): $150
Dining out and entertainment: $200
Personal care (gym membership, haircuts): $100
Savings and Goals:

Emergency fund: $200
Retirement savings: $200
Vacation fund: $100
Total Expenses: $2,800

In this budget, you have allocated a portion of your income towards all your essential expenses, such as rent, utilities, insurance, and debt payments. You have also accounted for variable expenses like groceries, transportation, and personal care. Importantly, you have dedicated funds for savings and specific goals like an emergency fund, retirement savings, and a vacation fund.

Now, let's see the potential savings impact of this budget:

Increased awareness: By tracking your expenses and income, you become aware of where your money is going and can identify areas where you may be overspending.

Prioritizing expenses: With a budget, you ensure that your essential expenses are covered first. This prevents overspending on discretionary items and helps you allocate funds towards savings goals.

Identifying cost-cutting opportunities: Reviewing your budget, you notice that you're spending a bit too much on dining out and entertainment. You decide to reduce this category to $150, saving $50 each month.

Building an emergency fund: By consistently saving $200 each month, your emergency fund grows over time, providing financial security and preventing the need for high-interest borrowing in case of unexpected expenses.

Retirement savings: By contributing $200 each month towards your retirement savings, you're building a nest egg for the future, taking advantage of compound interest and long-term growth potential.

Vacation fund: Saving $100 each month ensures that you have funds set aside specifically for a vacation, avoiding the need to rely on credit cards or dip into your emergency savings.

By following this budget, you are saving a total of $550 each month ($50 from dining out reduction, $200 for emergency fund, $200 for retirement, and $100 for vacation). Over the course of a year, your savings would amount to $6,600, not including any interest or investment returns.

This illustration demonstrates how a well-planned budget helps you allocate your income effectively, save money consistently, and work towards achieving your financial goals.

The 50/30/20 Budgeting

The 50/30/20 rule is much simpler than the golden ratio and is a simple planning strategy that can assist you with dealing with your money practically. The essential guideline is to partition your monthly income after tax into three spending categories 50% for needs , 30% for wants and 20% for investment funds or paying off debt.

Whatever budgeting ratio you use, always try to estimate the degree of action achieved during the budget period. At the end of each month, try to examine whether every one of the budgets had been achieved in real practice.

Let's assume you are earning $2,000 every month. This is what your saving plan could look like in the 50:30:20 budget ratio:

$1000 in your necessities or need envelopes.

$600 in your wanted envelopes.

$400 in your envelopes for reserve funds and debt reimbursement.

How using the 50/30/20 Budgeting can make you save

The 50/30/20 budgeting rule is a popular budgeting strategy that can help you save money and manage your finances effectively. It suggests allocating your after-tax income into three categories: needs, wants, and savings. Here's how it can help you save:

Needs (50%): Allocate 50% of your income to cover essential expenses such as housing, utilities, transportation, groceries, and minimum debt payments. This category focuses on your basic needs and ensures that you have a stable foundation for your budget.

Wants (30%): Dedicate 30% of your income to discretionary spending and non-essential expenses like dining out, entertainment, shopping, hobbies, and vacations. This category allows you to enjoy the things you desire without exceeding a reasonable portion of your income.

Savings (20%): Allocate 20% of your income towards savings and financial goals. This category includes building an emergency fund, paying off debt faster, saving for retirement, investing, or any other long-term financial objectives you may have.

By following the 50/30/20 budgeting rule, you create a structured framework that automatically prioritizes savings. Here's how it can lead to increased savings:

Clear allocation: The rule provides a clear guideline on how much to allocate towards your needs, wants, and savings. By setting aside a specific percentage for savings, you ensure that saving becomes a consistent and non-negotiable part of your budget.

Controlled spending: The 30% allocated to wants encourages you to be mindful of your discretionary spending. By keeping your wants within a set limit, you are less likely to overspend, which frees up more funds for savings.

Regular savings contributions: With a designated 20% for savings, you create a habit of consistent savings. By consistently setting aside a portion of your income, you gradually build up your savings over time.

Financial goals focus: The 20% allocated to savings helps you work towards achieving your financial goals. Whether it's saving for a down payment on a house, paying off debt, or investing for the future, this rule ensures that you allocate a significant portion of your income towards your long-term objectives.

Remember, the 50/30/20 budgeting rule is a guideline, and you can adjust the percentages to fit your personal situation. The key is to find a balance that allows you to cover your needs, enjoy your wants, and prioritize savings.

Increased awareness of spending: Implementing this budgeting rule requires tracking your expenses and categorizing them accordingly. This process increases your awareness of where your money is going and helps identify areas where you can make adjustments to save more. You may discover unnecessary expenses that can be reduced or eliminated, leading to more savings.

Emergency fund creation: The 20% allocated to savings can be used to build an emergency fund, which is crucial for financial security. Having an emergency fund helps cover unexpected expenses, such as medical bills or car repairs, without derailing your budget or going into debt. The 50/30/20 rule ensures that you consistently contribute to your emergency fund, gradually building it up over time.

Debt repayment: If you have debt, the 50/30/20 rule helps you allocate a portion of your income towards paying it off faster. By consistently dedicating a percentage of your income to debt repayment, you can accelerate the process of becoming debt-free. This reduces the amount of money spent on interest and frees up more funds for savings once the debt is eliminated.

Long-term financial security: The 50/30/20 rule emphasizes allocating a significant portion of your income towards savings and long-term financial goals.

By consistently saving and investing, you build wealth over time and set yourself up for a secure financial future. Whether it's saving for retirement, buying a home, or starting a business, this budgeting strategy ensures that you make progress towards your long-term objectives.

Flexibility and adjustment: While the 50/30/20 rule provides a general framework, it is flexible and can be adjusted based on your individual circumstances. If you want to save more aggressively, you can increase the percentage allocated to savings or decrease the percentage for wants. The key is to find a balance that allows you to cover your needs, enjoy your wants within reason, and save adequately.

By following the 50/30/20 budgeting rule and making conscious financial choices, you develop healthy financial habits and save money consistently. Over time, these savings can grow and provide you with a stronger financial foundation, increased peace of mind, and the ability to achieve your financial goals.

Illustration:

Let's illustrate how the 50/30/20 budgeting rule can work with a hypothetical monthly income of $4,000:

Needs (50%): Allocate 50% of your income to cover essential expenses.
Monthly Income: $4,000
Needs: 50% x $4,000 = $2,000

Examples of needs:

Rent or mortgage payment: $1,000
Utilities: $200
Transportation (car payment, fuel, insurance): $300
Groceries: $200
Minimum debt payments: $300
Wants (30%): Dedicate 30% of your income to discretionary spending and non-essential expenses.
Monthly Income: $4,000
Wants: 30% x $4,000 = $1,200

Examples of wants:

Dining out: $200
Entertainment (movies, concerts): $100
Shopping: $300
Hobbies: $200
Vacation savings: $400
Savings (20%): Allocate 20% of your income towards savings and financial goals.
Monthly Income: $4,000
Savings: 20% x $4,000 = $800

Examples of savings:

Emergency fund: $300
Retirement savings: $300
Debt repayment (above minimum payments): $200
By following this budgeting rule, you would allocate
$2,000 for needs, $1,200 for wants, and $800 for
savings each month.

This illustration shows that you are consistently
saving 20% of your income, which can help you build
an emergency fund, save for retirement, and make
progress towards your financial goals. It also provides
a clear allocation of your income and helps you
prioritize your spending while ensuring that you cover
your essential expenses.

Keep in mind that these numbers are just examples,
and you can adjust the percentages based on your
income and financial situation. The key is to create a
budget that aligns with your goals and allows you to
save effectively.

Cash stuffing

Cash stuffing is a budget and saving method wherein
you pull out cash toward the beginning of the month
(or at whatever point you get a pay) and afterward put

certain sums in envelopes marked with explicit classifications. The thought is that it will hold you back from spending more than you have planned for that budget.

Cash stuffing is the trending interpretation of the well established 'envelope system of savings – taking money and stuffing envelopes, or organizers, or anything you desire to use, for various classes of expenditure in your monthly savings plan.

The reason why money stuffing is really smart is because it tends to make people stop their spending once they reach the amount of money in the envelope or be mindful of their spending when they realize the amount in the envelope is going down.

However, you should be mindful of where you keep your envelopes so that it will not get stolen, lost or thrown away by a novice.

To begin cash stuffing, take a couple of envelopes, write a particular budget class on every one. For instance you can have a 'films' envelope, a 'cafés' envelope and a 'drinks' envelope and afterward put the cash you intend to spend on those things into the envelopes.

The envelope saving approach otherwise called 'cash stuffing' depends on money and envelopes to design spending.

With the envelope system, you designate your salary toward explicit classifications by putting cash in named envelopes.

The method that I am using that is similar to that of cash stuffing using envelopes is that I divided my proposed expenditure for the month into 4 different bank accounts, the money in each bank is the one I will spend for the week and it works because it helps me to be mindful of my spending.

This envelope system has been around for a really long time, however cash stuffing or the envelope saving is gaining new momentum in recent times.

The idea is basic: Take a couple of envelopes, categorize each based on expenses and stuff with cash.

Over the years, people have utilized the envelope framework consistently, using genuine money and envelopes. But now, people are using advanced and modern techniques such as apps.

The envelope system of cash stuffing is so successful since It shows you at that moment in time how much cash is going into different variable costs and you will feel a profound bond with your cash as well. Since cash is noticeable, accessible and lives with you, it's simpler to know about the amount you're spending and you're probably going to spend short of what you would with a card, though this depends on your nature.

The envelope system can help new budgeters and hasty spenders. It allows you to put forth objectives and check the amount you spend and save. This type of cash stuffing is good for individuals who need to assume responsibility for their funds in an active manner.

How cash stuffing can help save money

Cash stuffing is a method of saving money that involves physically setting aside cash in a designated location, such as a jar or envelope. While it may not be as effective as other saving strategies like investing or opening a savings account, it can still offer some benefits. Here are a few ways cash stuffing can help save money:

Budgeting and visual tracking: Cash stuffing allows you to allocate a specific amount of money for savings, giving you a tangible representation of your progress. Seeing the pile of cash grow can serve as a visual reminder of your savings goals, which can motivate you to continue saving.

Reducing impulsive spending: By using cash for daily expenses instead of relying solely on electronic payments, you can become more conscious of your spending habits. When you physically see the money leaving your wallet, you may be less likely to make impulsive purchases, helping you save money in the long run.

Emergency fund: Cash stuffing can be particularly useful for creating an emergency fund. Keeping a stash of cash at home can provide a financial safety net in case of unexpected events, such as a power outage or temporary loss of access to banking services.

Saving loose change: Cash stuffing often involves saving loose change. Collecting and setting aside loose change on a regular basis can add up over time, providing you with additional savings without much effort.

Avoiding fees: Cash transactions can help you avoid certain fees. For example, if you use cash for small purchases instead of using a debit or credit card, you can avoid potential transaction fees or minimum purchase requirements.

While cash stuffing can be a helpful tool for some people, it's important to note that it also carries some risks. Cash stored at home may be vulnerable to theft or loss in the event of a fire or natural disaster. Additionally, cash does not earn interest, which means its value may erode over time due to inflation. Therefore, it's generally recommended to consider other saving options, such as a bank account or investment vehicles, for long-term savings goals.

Building discipline and mindfulness: Cash stuffing requires discipline and mindfulness in managing your expenses. It encourages you to make intentional choices about where and how you spend your money. By physically handling cash and making conscious decisions about how much to set aside, you can develop better financial habits and improve your overall money management skills.

Limiting unnecessary spending: When you have a limited amount of cash available, you're more likely to think twice before making non-essential purchases. This can help you prioritize your needs over wants and curb impulse buying. Cash stuffing forces you to live within your means, which can contribute to long-term financial stability and prevent unnecessary debt.

Teaching children about money: Cash stuffing can be an effective method for teaching children about saving and money management. By involving them in the process and encouraging them to set aside cash for specific goals, such as buying a toy or saving for a trip, you can instill valuable financial lessons early on.

Supplementing other saving methods: Cash stuffing can be used in conjunction with other saving methods. For example, you can allocate a portion of your cash stuffing savings towards an interest-earning bank account or investment portfolio. This way, you can benefit from the advantages of both physical cash savings and the potential growth offered by traditional saving or investment avenues.

Psychological benefits: Some individuals find the act of physically handling and saving cash more satisfying and motivating than purely digital or abstract methods. The tangible nature of cash can provide a sense of accomplishment and progress as the stack grows, which can contribute to a positive saving mindset.

Remember, while cash stuffing can be a useful tool for some, it's essential to assess your specific financial situation and goals. Consider the potential risks and limitations of relying solely on cash stuffing for long-term savings and explore other options to make your savings more effective, such as opening a savings account, investing, or utilizing automated saving tools.

Illustration:

Mary was a young professional who wants to develop better saving habits. She decides to try cash stuffing as a strategy to reach her financial goals. Here's how it unfolds:

Setting a savings goal: Mary identifies her goal to save $500 within three months for a vacation. She breaks it down into weekly targets, aiming to save around $42 each week.

Cash stuffing implementation: Mary designates a jar specifically for her cash stuffing savings. At the end of each week, she withdraws $42 in cash from her bank account and puts it in the jar.

Visual progress and motivation: As Mary consistently adds cash to the jar, she sees it accumulate over time. Witnessing the growing stack of money acts as a visual representation of her progress, serving as a source of motivation and reinforcing her commitment to saving.

Conscious spending habits: With her cash-only approach, Mary becomes more conscious of her spending habits. When she goes shopping or dines out, she carefully considers her purchases, opting for essential items and minimizing impulsive spending. The physical exchange of cash makes her more aware of the money leaving her possession, discouraging unnecessary expenses.

Supplementing with loose change: Mary also saves loose change and adds it to her cash stuffing jar. She regularly empties her pockets and wallet into a separate container, collecting coins. Over time, these small contributions gradually increase her savings, providing an additional boost to her overall goal.

Emergency fund creation: In addition to her vacation savings, Mary decides to allocate a portion of her cash stuffing towards building an emergency fund. She sets aside $20 each week from her cash savings specifically for unexpected expenses, ensuring she has a safety net in case of emergencies.

Achieving the savings goal: By diligently sticking to her weekly cash stuffing routine, managing her expenses, and saving loose change, Mary successfully reaches her savings goal of $500 within the designated three-month period. She feels proud of her accomplishment and is excited to use her savings for the vacation she planned.

This illustration showcases how cash stuffing, coupled with conscious spending habits and specific savings goals, can help individuals like Mary achieve their objectives. The visual progress, mindful spending, and disciplined approach contribute to building a healthy savings habit and financial stability over time.

Tandem saving and spending

In this hack, saving and spending remain closely connected. In basic words, you save as much as you spend. For instance, if you spend $3000 in a month, you will save the same $3000 in your monthly savings. This hacking strategy is most suitable for high earners and middle class people. However, anyone can think about this hack and see if you can adopt it.

Tandem saving and spending can also be suitable for people that receive daily pay. What is important is to find a suitable budget plan and saving hack that suits your own income range and lifestyle.

How tandem saving and spending can help you save

Tandem saving and spending is a concept that involves coordinating your saving and spending activities to maximize your savings potential. It emphasizes a balanced approach to managing your finances by aligning your saving goals with your spending habits. Here are a few ways tandem saving and spending can help you save:

Budgeting: Tandem saving and spending begins with creating a budget that accounts for both your income and expenses. By tracking your spending, you can identify areas where you can cut back and allocate more funds towards your savings goals. It helps you prioritize your expenses and ensures that you save a portion of your income before spending on non-essential items.

Automated savings: Set up automatic transfers from your checking account to a savings account each time you receive a paycheck. By making saving a priority and automating the process, you remove the temptation to spend that money elsewhere. This approach helps you consistently save without having to rely on willpower alone.

Pay yourself first: When you receive income, allocate a certain percentage or fixed amount towards your savings before allocating funds for other expenses. By prioritizing saving at the beginning, you ensure that your savings goals are met and adjust your spending accordingly.

Curb impulsive spending: Tandem saving and spending involves being mindful of your spending habits. Before making a purchase, ask yourself if it aligns with your financial goals and if it's a necessary expense. By curbing impulsive spending, you free up more funds to save.

Find ways to save on expenses: Tandem saving and spending encourages you to actively seek opportunities to reduce your expenses. Look for ways to save on utilities, transportation, groceries, and other regular expenses. Consider alternatives and make conscious choices that allow you to maintain your desired lifestyle while saving money.

Set specific goals: Define clear saving goals, whether it's building an emergency fund, saving for a down payment on a house, or planning for retirement. Having specific goals in mind helps you stay motivated and focused on saving. Break down your goals into smaller milestones, making it easier to track your progress and celebrate achievements along the way.

Review and adjust regularly: Regularly review your saving and spending habits to ensure they align with your goals. Assess your progress, make adjustments as needed, and identify areas where you can improve. This process helps you stay on track and optimize your saving potential.

By adopting a tandem saving and spending approach, you can strike a balance between enjoying your income and securing your financial future. It enables you to save consistently, make conscious spending choices, and work towards your long-term financial goals.

Track your progress: Keep a record of your saving and spending activities. Use personal finance apps or spreadsheets to track your income, expenses, and savings. Regularly reviewing your financial records allows you to identify patterns, track your progress, and make informed decisions about your saving and spending habits.

Prioritize debt repayment: If you have outstanding debts, such as credit card debt or loans, prioritize paying them off. High-interest debt can eat into your savings potential. By tackling your debts, you not only save money on interest payments but also free up more funds for saving once the debts are paid off.

Maximize rewards and discounts: Take advantage of rewards programs, coupons, and discounts whenever possible. Whether it's using cashback credit cards, loyalty programs, or taking advantage of sales and promotions, these strategies help you save money on your regular purchases. Consider saving the money you would have spent and redirecting it towards your savings goals.

Evaluate recurring expenses: Review your recurring expenses, such as subscriptions, memberships, and services. Determine if you're getting sufficient value from each expense. Cancel or downgrade any subscriptions or services that you no longer need or use. Redirect the saved money towards your savings.

Practice delayed gratification: Instead of making impulse purchases, practice delaying gratification. Give yourself time to consider whether a purchase is necessary or if it aligns with your financial goals. Often, taking a pause allows you to make more mindful decisions and avoid unnecessary spending.

Find ways to increase your income: Consider exploring opportunities to increase your income. This could involve taking on a side job, freelancing, starting a small business, or investing in income-generating assets. Increasing your income provides more room for saving while still enjoying your lifestyle.

Seek financial advice: If you're uncertain about the best strategies for saving and spending, consider seeking guidance from a financial advisor. They can provide personalized advice tailored to your financial situation, help you set realistic goals, and offer strategies to optimize your savings.

Remember, the key to tandem saving and spending is finding a balance that works for you. It's about being intentional with your financial decisions and consistently saving while still enjoying your income. By practicing these strategies and staying focused on your goals, you can build a strong foundation for long-term financial security.

Illustration:
Let's consider an example to illustrate how tandem saving and spending can help you save.

Tina a working professional who wants to save for a down payment on a house. Here's how she implements tandem saving and spending:

Budgeting: Tina creates a monthly budget that includes all her income sources and expenses. She categorizes her expenses into necessities (rent, utilities, groceries) and discretionary spending (eating out, entertainment). She realizes that she can reduce her discretionary spending to allocate more funds toward savings.

Automated savings: Tina sets up an automatic transfer of 20% of her monthly income from her checking account to a dedicated savings account. This ensures that she consistently saves a portion of her earnings before spending on other items.

Pay yourself first: Whenever Tina receives her paycheck, she immediately transfers a fixed amount into her savings account, treating it as paying herself first. This way, she ensures that her savings are a priority.

Curb impulsive spending: Before making any non-essential purchase, Tina asks herself if it aligns with her goal of saving for a down payment. She becomes more mindful of her spending habits and avoids unnecessary purchases.

Find ways to save on expenses: Tina starts seeking opportunities to reduce her expenses. She switches to energy-efficient appliances, compares prices at different grocery stores, and cooks meals at home instead of eating out. These changes help her save money on her regular expenses.

Set specific goals: Tina sets a specific target of saving $40,000 for her down payment within two years. She breaks it down into smaller milestones of saving $1,666 per month. Having clear goals keeps her motivated and focused on saving consistently.

Review and adjust regularly: Tina reviews her budget and spending habits every month. She identifies areas where she can further cut back on expenses and adjust her budget accordingly. She celebrates her milestones along the way, such as reaching the halfway mark or achieving a certain savings amount.

By following these strategies, Tina successfully practices tandem saving and spending. Over time, she accumulates the necessary funds for her down payment. Through conscious spending choices and consistent saving efforts, she achieves her goal of homeownership while maintaining financial stability.

Remember, this is just an illustration, and your own saving and spending journey will be unique to your financial goals and circumstances.

Power of Pausing

As the name implies, this is the act of pausing to think twice before you make a purchase decision on something you don't plan for.

For instance, when you are walking and you see something that attracts you, the power of pausing says you should not get it immediately. You should go to where you are going and later decide whether you really need it or not.

Also, let say while shopping online, you see something that you like but is not planned for, don't get it immediately. Put it in the cart for a few days and then decide whether to buy it or not. This hack assists you with keeping away from superfluous spending.

How power of pausing can help you save

The power of pausing can be a valuable tool when it comes to saving money. Here are a few ways in which the act of pausing can contribute to your savings:

Impulse buying: Pausing before making a purchase can prevent you from succumbing to impulse buying. Many times, we're tempted to buy things on a whim without considering whether we truly need them. By taking a pause, you give yourself time to reflect on the necessity of the purchase, evaluate its value, and determine if it aligns with your financial goals. This simple pause can help you avoid unnecessary expenses and save money in the long run.

Budgeting and planning: Pausing also plays a crucial role in budgeting and financial planning. Before making any major financial decisions, such as investing in stocks, buying a car, or taking on additional debt, it's important to pause and thoroughly assess the potential impact on your finances. By taking the time to research, analyze, and weigh the pros and cons, you can make more informed choices that align with your financial objectives. This can prevent costly mistakes and contribute to your overall savings.

Comparison shopping: Pausing allows you to shop around and compare prices before making a purchase. By taking a moment to pause and explore different options, you can identify the best deals, discounts, or sales available. This way, you can avoid overspending and ensure that you're getting the most value for your money. Comparison shopping can be particularly useful for big-ticket items or ongoing expenses like insurance premiums, where even a small reduction in costs can lead to significant long-term savings.

Delayed gratification: The power of pausing also ties into the concept of delayed gratification. Rather than instantly indulging in a purchase or experience, you can pause and consider whether it's something you truly need or if it can be postponed. By practicing delayed gratification, you can avoid unnecessary expenses and save money for more meaningful or important goals, such as building an emergency fund, paying off debt, or investing for the future.

In summary, the act of pausing can help you save money by avoiding impulse buying, aiding in budgeting and planning, enabling comparison shopping, and practicing delayed gratification. By taking a moment to pause and reflect on your financial decisions, you can make more intentional choices that align with your long-term savings goals.

Avoiding subscription traps: In the era of subscription services, it's easy to accumulate multiple subscriptions without realizing the financial impact. Pausing before subscribing to a new service or renewing an existing one allows you to reassess your needs. Take the time to evaluate whether you're getting sufficient value from each subscription and consider canceling or downgrading any that are underutilized or no longer necessary. This can help you cut down on monthly expenses and save money over time.

Negotiating better deals: When making a significant purchase or entering into a contract, pausing can give you the opportunity to negotiate better terms. By taking the time to research and gather information about alternative options, prices, or competitors, you can approach negotiations from a position of knowledge and leverage. This pause allows you to explore potential discounts, promotions, or bargaining points, ultimately helping you secure a better deal and potentially saving you a substantial amount of money.

Energy conservation: Pausing and being mindful of your energy usage can lead to cost savings. By simply pausing to turn off lights, unplug electronics when not in use, adjust thermostats, or optimize heating and cooling settings, you can reduce your utility bills. Additionally, pausing before upgrading to energy-efficient appliances or making home improvements can help you prioritize investments that offer the greatest long-term energy savings, further contributing to your financial well-being.

Avoiding unnecessary fees: Pausing before making financial transactions or taking actions that may incur fees can save you money. For example, withdrawing cash from an out-of-network ATM often comes with fees, so taking a pause to find a fee-free option can prevent unnecessary charges. Similarly, carefully reviewing bank statements, credit card bills, and invoices can help identify any erroneous charges or fees that can be disputed or rectified, ultimately saving you money.

Remember, the power of pausing is not about completely denying yourself or being overly frugal. It's about making deliberate and thoughtful decisions that align with your financial goals and priorities. By incorporating this practice into your everyday life, you can cultivate a habit of conscious spending, which in turn helps you save money and build a more secure financial future.

Illustration:

Let's consider an illustration of how the power of pausing can help you save money:

Imagine you're in a store and come across a new gadget that catches your eye. It's the latest model with all the bells and whistles, and you're tempted to buy it on the spot. However, you decide to pause before making the purchase.

During this pause, you ask yourself a few important questions: Do you really need this gadget? Will it significantly improve your life or fulfill a specific purpose? Can you afford it without compromising your other financial goals?

As you reflect on these questions, you realize that while the gadget seems exciting, it's not a necessity. You have a similar device that functions perfectly fine, and purchasing the new one would be more of a luxury than a practical investment.

By pausing and considering your options, you decide to hold off on buying the gadget for now. Instead, you choose to allocate the funds towards paying off your credit card debt, which will save you from accruing additional interest charges. This decision aligns with your long-term financial goal of becoming debt-free.

A few months later, you come across a limited-time promotion for the same gadget. This time, however, you're better prepared. You remember the pause you took earlier, and you decide to do some research before jumping into a purchase.

During your research, you discover that there are alternative brands offering similar features at a lower price point. You compare prices, read customer reviews, and assess the overall value each option provides.

By taking this pause and engaging in comparison shopping, you find a more affordable alternative that meets your needs just as well. You purchase the gadget at a significant discount compared to the initial price you encountered. The money you save from making a more informed decision can now be allocated towards your emergency fund or invested for future financial growth.

In this illustration, the power of pausing allowed you to resist impulse buying, evaluate your financial priorities, and make informed choices. By exercising patience and thoughtful consideration, you avoided unnecessary expenses, saved money, and took steps toward achieving your broader financial objectives.

Remember, each situation is unique, and the power of pausing can be applied to various aspects of your financial life. It's a tool that empowers you to make intentional decisions that align with your goals, ultimately leading to improved financial well-being and increased savings.

Be practical

Perhaps the greatest error one could make when making a saving plan or budget is to attempt to spend a specific sum every month that is just not practical or in other words planning to spend money far lower to your weekly or monthly average spending.

Setting a budget that is in accordance with your ongoing spending is an effective method for refocusing and coordinating. Afterwards, you can change the financial plan to lessen spending in specific classes to assist you with saving more.

You should also design your budget around what you knew would spring up that month. Each is different, so do your spending. Some months, you will spend more and save less while the reverse is the case in other months.

How being practical can help you save till you get rich and beyond

Being practical can indeed help you save money in various ways. Here are some practical tips to help you save:

Budgeting: Creating a budget is a practical way to manage your finances effectively. It allows you to track your income and expenses, identify areas where you can cut back, and allocate money towards savings goals.

Differentiating needs from wants: Being practical involves prioritizing your needs over wants. By distinguishing between essential expenses (such as housing, utilities, and groceries) and discretionary spending (such as entertainment and dining out), you can focus on fulfilling your necessities and save money by reducing unnecessary purchases.

Comparison shopping: Practical individuals often compare prices before making a purchase. Whether you're buying groceries, electronics, or other goods, researching and comparing prices at different stores or online platforms can help you find the best deals and save money.

Reducing energy consumption: Adopting practical habits like turning off lights when not in use, using energy-efficient appliances, and properly insulating your home can significantly reduce your energy bills. These small adjustments not only save money but also contribute to environmental sustainability.

Meal planning and cooking at home: Eating out or ordering takeout regularly can be costly. By planning your meals, making a shopping list, and preparing food at home, you can save money on dining expenses and potentially eat healthier too.

Avoiding impulsive purchases: Practical individuals tend to avoid impulsive buying decisions. Before making a purchase, take some time to consider if it's necessary and fits within your budget. Delaying purchases can help you determine if you truly need the item or if it was just an impulse.

Building an emergency fund: Practicality involves preparing for unexpected financial situations. Set aside a portion of your income regularly into an emergency fund. Having a financial cushion can help you avoid going into debt or relying on credit cards during emergencies.

Utilizing discounts, coupons, and rewards: Take advantage of discounts, coupons, and loyalty programs offered by retailers. This practical approach allows you to save money on regular purchases and earn rewards that can be used for future savings.

DIY projects: If you have the necessary skills and resources, consider tackling do-it-yourself (DIY) projects instead of hiring professionals. Whether it's minor repairs, home improvements, or basic maintenance tasks, taking a practical approach and doing it yourself can save you money on labor costs.

Long-term thinking: Being practical means considering the long-term benefits and costs of your decisions. Instead of seeking immediate gratification, think about the long-term consequences. For example, investing in quality products that last longer may initially cost more but can save you money in the long run by avoiding frequent replacements.

By adopting practical habits and incorporating these tips into your daily life, you can make significant progress in saving money and achieving your financial goals.

Illustration:

Meet Nike, a practical individual who wants to save money. Here's how she applies practicality in her daily life:

Budgeting: Nike creates a monthly budget to track her income and expenses. She identifies areas where she can reduce spending, such as cutting back on eating out and entertainment expenses.

Meal planning and cooking at home: Nike plans her meals for the week, makes a shopping list, and buys groceries in bulk. By cooking at home and bringing her lunch to work instead of eating out, she saves a significant amount of money on dining expenses.

Comparison shopping: When Nike needs to purchase a new laptop, she researches different brands, models, and prices. By comparing prices at various stores and online platforms, she finds a great deal that saves her money without compromising on quality.

Utilizing discounts and rewards: Nike signs up for loyalty programs at her favorite stores and regularly checks for discounts and coupons. She uses these rewards and discounts to save money on clothing, household items, and other purchases.

DIY projects: Nike is handy with tools and enjoys taking on DIY projects. Instead of hiring a professional for a minor home repair, she tackles it herself, saving money on labor costs.

Energy conservation: Nike takes practical steps to conserve energy, such as turning off lights and appliances when not in use, using energy-efficient light bulbs, and adjusting her thermostat. As a result, her energy bills decrease, leading to long-term savings.

Long-term thinking: Sarah invests in a durable, energy-efficient washing machine, even though it costs more upfront. Over time, the machine's efficiency and longevity save her money on repairs and replacements.

Building an emergency fund: Sarah sets aside a portion of her income each month into an emergency fund. This practical habit provides her with financial security and helps her avoid debt when unexpected expenses arise.

By incorporating these practical strategies into her life, Nike successfully saves money and achieves her financial goals. She feels more in control of her finances and has a sense of financial security for the future.

Check your plan routinely

The craft of making a saving plan can be both time and energy consuming. You should not copy another person's savings plan, rather use your own lifestyle and income to craft your budget.

After you have drafted your saving plan and have started saving, checking your savings and spending will help you to monitor your spending on a regular basis. You can set a time you will be checking your budget. You can set daily, weekly or monthly to absorb how your spending for the month is looking. This assists you with being more mindful of what is happening monetarily and not getting astounded or stunned toward the week's end by any expenses you didn't expect.

How checking your plan routinely can help you save money till you get rich and beyond

Checking your plan routinely can help you save money in several ways:

Identify unnecessary expenses: By reviewing your plan regularly, you can identify any unnecessary expenses that can be eliminated or reduced. This could include subscriptions you no longer use, services you no longer need, or recurring charges that you can do without. By cutting these expenses, you can save money each month.

Catch billing errors: Mistakes can happen, and sometimes you may be charged for services you didn't use or at a higher rate than agreed upon. By regularly checking your plan and comparing it with your bills or statements, you can catch any billing errors and have them corrected. This can help you avoid paying for something you shouldn't and keep your costs in check.

Optimize your plans: Service providers often update their plans and offer new features or discounts. By reviewing your plan periodically, you can ensure that you are on the most cost-effective plan for your needs. You might find that your current plan no longer suits your requirements and switching to a different plan or provider could save you money.

Take advantage of promotions and discounts: Companies frequently offer promotional deals and discounts to attract new customers or retain existing ones. By routinely checking your plan, you can stay informed about these offers and take advantage of them when they align with your needs. This can result in substantial savings over time.

Evaluate alternatives: By regularly reviewing your plan, you can assess whether there are better alternatives available in the market. This is particularly relevant for services like insurance, utilities, or internet providers, where there may be competing companies offering similar services at lower prices or with better terms. Comparing options and making informed decisions can help you save money.

Track your progress: Checking your plan routinely allows you to track your financial progress and monitor your spending habits. It helps you stay aware of where your money is going and identify areas where you may need to make adjustments. This awareness can lead to smarter financial decisions and better control over your expenses.

In summary, checking your plan routinely can help you identify unnecessary expenses, catch billing errors, optimize your plans, take advantage of promotions and discounts, evaluate alternatives, and track your progress. By actively managing your finances in this way, you can save money and make more informed decisions about your spending.

Illustration:

Let's consider an illustration to demonstrate how checking your plan routinely can help you save money:

Meet Foluke, a budget-conscious individual who decides to review her expenses and plans regularly to optimize her finances. Here's how her routine check helps her save money:

Identifying unnecessary expenses: During her review, Foluke discovers that she has a gym membership that she rarely uses. By canceling it, she saves $40 per month, which amounts to $480 per year.

Catching billing errors: While going through her credit card statement, Foluke notices that her internet service provider has been charging her an extra $10 for the past three months. She contacts the provider, gets the error rectified, and saves $30.

Optimizing plans: Foluke realizes that she has been on the same mobile phone plan for a while. Upon researching, she finds a comparable plan with another provider that offers more data and minutes at a lower cost. By switching providers, she saves $20 per month, which amounts to $240 per year.

Taking advantage of promotions and discounts: During her routine check, Foluke comes across a promotional offer from her insurance provider. By switching to a different plan with the same coverage but at a discounted rate, she saves $50 per month, amounting to $600 per year.

Evaluating alternatives: Foluke discovers that her current electricity provider has higher rates compared to other providers in her area. By switching to a different provider, she saves an average of $15 per month, which amounts to $180 per year.

Tracking progress: Foluke maintains a spreadsheet to track her expenses and savings. By regularly reviewing her plan and monitoring her progress, she identifies areas where she can make further adjustments. For example, she notices that her streaming subscriptions are costing her more than she anticipated. By canceling a few subscriptions, she saves an additional $20 per month, amounting to $240 per year.

In total, by routinely checking her plans and making adjustments, Foluke saves $1,770 per year. These savings accumulate over time and provide her with extra funds that she can allocate towards her financial goals, such as building an emergency fund, paying off debt, or investing for the future.

By incorporating a habit of reviewing her plans periodically, Foluke continues to make smart financial decisions, optimize her expenses, and maintain control over her finances, ultimately leading to long-term savings and financial stability.

Be adjustable

Some people believe that they must be rigidly strict for them to achieve their savings but this is not true. The most constant thing is change. So you need to design your budget in a way that you will be able to adjust your spending and savings in accordance to what is happening at that point in time.

Assuming you overspend on the transport budget but underspend on your food budget, you can adjust by moving money from one budget to the other.

Remain strict with the sum you've planned to spend for that month, however be more relaxed about where precisely that cash is going.

How being adjustable can make you save money till you get rich and beyond

Being adjustable can indeed help you save money in various ways. Here are a few examples:

Utility bills: By adjusting your energy consumption habits, you can significantly reduce your utility bills. Simple actions like turning off lights when not in use, adjusting the thermostat, using energy-efficient appliances, and being mindful of water usage can lead to substantial savings over time.

Subscription services: Many subscription services offer different plans or tiers based on your needs. By adjusting your subscription plans to match your actual usage, you can avoid paying for features or services you don't need. For example, streaming platforms often have options for different video quality or simultaneous streams, allowing you to choose a plan that aligns with your preferences and budget.

Transportation costs: If you have flexibility in your daily commute, adjusting your travel schedule can help you save money. Avoiding peak hours or using public transportation during off-peak times can reduce expenses on fuel, tolls, and parking fees. Additionally, carpooling or ridesharing with others can further cut down on transportation costs.

Insurance premiums: Insurance providers often offer adjustable policies that allow you to modify coverage levels and deductibles. By assessing your needs and adjusting your insurance policies accordingly, you can find a balance between adequate coverage and affordable premiums. For example, increasing your car insurance deductible can lower your monthly premium, saving you money in the long run if you're a safe driver.

Food and groceries: Adjusting your eating habits and meal planning can lead to significant savings. Cooking at home instead of dining out, buying groceries in bulk or on sale, and avoiding food waste by properly utilizing leftovers can all contribute to reducing your overall food expenses.

Entertainment and leisure activities: Rather than spending money on costly outings or activities, consider exploring free or low-cost alternatives. Many cities offer free community events, parks, museums with discounted or free admission days, and recreational facilities that provide affordable options for leisure and entertainment.

Flexible budgeting: Having an adjustable budget allows you to adapt your spending habits based on your financial goals and circumstances. By regularly reviewing your expenses and identifying areas where you can cut back or make adjustments, you can allocate more funds towards savings, investments, or paying off debts, ultimately helping you save money in the long term.

Remember, being adjustable doesn't necessarily mean sacrificing quality or enjoyment. It's about making conscious choices and optimizing your resources to align with your priorities and financial objectives.

Illustration:

Let's illustrate an example of how being adjustable can help you save money:

Meet Ronke, a budget-conscious individual who wants to reduce her monthly expenses. Here's how being adjustable benefits her:

Utility bills: Ronke takes proactive steps to conserve energy. She adjusts her thermostat settings, switches to energy-efficient light bulbs, and unplugs electronic devices when not in use. As a result, her monthly electricity bill decreases by 20%.

Subscription services: Ronke reviews her various subscription services and realizes she's paying for features she rarely uses. She adjusts her streaming plan to a lower tier that still meets her entertainment needs, saving $15 per month.

Transportation costs: Ronke typically drives during peak traffic hours, resulting in higher fuel costs and increased wear and tear on her vehicle. She decides to adjust her work schedule, commuting during off-peak hours when traffic is lighter. This change reduces her monthly fuel expenses by 15%.

Food and groceries: Ronke starts planning her meals ahead of time, making a shopping list and buying groceries in bulk when they are on sale. By avoiding impulsive purchases and utilizing leftovers effectively, she reduces her monthly food expenses by 10%.

Entertainment and leisure activities: Ronke explores free community events, visits local parks, and takes advantage of discounted admission days at museums. Instead of costly outings, she finds joy in these affordable or free alternatives, saving $50 per month.

By implementing these adjustments, Ronke saves a total of $150 per month. Over the course of a year, this amounts to $1,800 in savings.

This illustration showcases how being adjustable in different aspects of life can lead to tangible financial benefits. By making conscious choices and adapting to more cost-effective options, Ronke successfully reduces her monthly expenses without compromising on her quality of life.

Plan for emergency costs

You must have an emergency plan in your savings to succeed. If you don't have emergency savings, you would always be frustrated whenever an emergency cost happened that you didn't anticipate which might prompt you to forsake your savings plan. Since, we can't know everything that could occur during the month, setting aside certain bucks for any emergency costs can assist you to remain steadfast with your financial plan.

If you have emergency savings, you feel less strain and nervous if something happens that you didn't anticipate. You will just pull the cash from that emergency savings and if not enough you will supplement the remainder of that cost from your main savings account.

How planning for emergency costs can make you save till you get rich and beyond

Planning for emergency costs can indeed help you save money in the long run. Here's how:

Building an emergency fund: One of the primary ways to plan for emergency costs is by creating an emergency fund. This fund is a dedicated savings account specifically for unexpected expenses such as medical bills, car repairs, or job loss. By regularly contributing to your emergency fund, you'll be prepared for unforeseen circumstances without having to rely on credit cards or loans. Having an emergency fund helps you avoid high-interest debt and the stress associated with financial emergencies.

Budgeting for emergencies: Another aspect of planning for emergency costs is budgeting. When creating your monthly budget, allocate a portion of your income towards emergency savings. Treating your emergency fund as a fixed expense ensures that you prioritize saving for unforeseen circumstances. By including emergency savings in your budget, you're effectively setting aside money for emergencies rather than spending it on non-essential items.

Avoiding unnecessary expenses: When you have a plan for emergencies, you're more likely to be conscious of your spending habits. You'll be motivated to differentiate between essential and non-essential expenses, making it easier to avoid unnecessary purchases. By cutting back on discretionary spending, you can redirect those funds to your emergency savings. This disciplined approach can help you save a significant amount over time.

Lowering insurance premiums: Having appropriate insurance coverage is crucial for financial protection in emergencies. However, you can also save by reviewing your insurance policies and finding ways to lower your premiums without compromising on coverage. For example, you can increase your deductibles, bundle multiple policies for discounts, or shop around for better rates. By reducing your insurance costs, you'll have more money available for emergency savings.

Being proactive with maintenance: Regularly maintaining your home, car, or other assets can help prevent major breakdowns or expensive repairs. By performing routine maintenance and addressing minor issues promptly, you can avoid emergency situations that might otherwise lead to unexpected costs. Being proactive and investing in preventive maintenance can save you money in the long run.

Researching and comparing prices: In the event of an emergency, it's essential to make informed decisions and not overspend on immediate solutions. By researching and comparing prices for necessary services or repairs, you can find the best deals or negotiate better rates. Taking the time to explore options and seek competitive pricing can help you save money when emergencies arise.

In summary, planning for emergency costs allows you to save money by creating an emergency fund, budgeting for emergencies, avoiding unnecessary expenses, lowering insurance premiums, being proactive with maintenance, and researching prices. By having a financial cushion and adopting smart money management strategies, you'll be better prepared for emergencies while also building long-term savings.

Illustration:

Let's consider an illustration to better understand how planning for emergency costs can help you save.

Meet Toyin, a responsible individual who decides to plan for emergency costs.

Step 1: Building an emergency fund
Toyin starts by setting up an emergency fund. She determines that she wants to have at least three months' worth of living expenses saved in case of unforeseen circumstances. After evaluating her monthly expenses, she calculates that her living expenses amount to $2,500 per month. Therefore, Sarah sets a goal to save $7,500 in her emergency fund.

Step 2: Budgeting for emergencies
Toyin includes her emergency savings as a fixed expense in her monthly budget. She decides to allocate $250 from her monthly income toward her emergency fund. This disciplined approach ensures that Toyin prioritizes saving for emergencies and reduces the likelihood of spending that money on non-essential items.

Step 3: Avoiding unnecessary expenses
Toyin takes a closer look at her spending habits and identifies areas where she can cut back on discretionary expenses. She decides to reduce her dining out budget and limit her entertainment expenses. By making these conscious choices, Toyin can redirect an additional $100 per month towards her emergency fund.

Step 4: Lowering insurance premiums
Toyin reviews her insurance policies and contacts her providers to explore opportunities for savings. She discovers that by increasing her deductibles slightly and bundling her auto and home insurance policies, she can save $50 per month on her premiums. Toyin redirects this amount to her emergency fund as well.

Step 5: Being proactive with maintenance
Toyin understands the importance of regular

maintenance to prevent emergencies and unexpected expenses. She schedules routine maintenance for her car, such as oil changes and tire rotations, which cost her $50 every three months. By investing in preventive maintenance, she avoids costly breakdowns that could potentially disrupt her budget.

Step 6: Researching and comparing prices
In a hypothetical scenario, Toyin's water heater breaks down, and she needs to get it repaired or replaced urgently. Instead of opting for the first available service provider, Toyin takes the time to research and compare prices. She obtains multiple quotes and manages to find a reputable plumber who offers the necessary service at a lower cost, saving her $200 compared to the initial quote.

By implementing these strategies, Toyin successfully builds her emergency fund and manages to save money:

Monthly contribution to emergency fund: $250
Reduced discretionary expenses: $100
Savings from lowered insurance premiums: $50
Prevented emergency expenses through maintenance: $0
Savings from researching and comparing prices: $200
In a year, Sarah would have saved $3,600 ($300 per

month) in her emergency fund, plus an additional $350 from reduced expenses, insurance savings, and better pricing. Over time, this disciplined approach allows Toyin to accumulate a substantial emergency fund while also enjoying overall financial stability.

Remember, everyone's financial situation and emergency needs are unique. Adjust your savings goals, budget, and strategies according to your circumstances to make the most out of your emergency planning and savings.

Learn to say no

To have savings you must learn how to say no to certain expenses, especially ones that are not necessary at that particular point in time. You should have penned down important stuff you wanted to buy for that month in your budget. This will make it easier for you to say no to any impromptu expenses.

How learning to say no can help you save till you get rich and beyond

Learning to say no can indeed help you save in various aspects of life. Here are a few ways saying no can contribute to your savings:

Financial Decisions: By learning to say no to unnecessary expenses, impulsive purchases, or extravagant outings, you can maintain better control over your finances. This can help you prioritize your spending, cut down on non-essential items, and save money for future goals or emergencies.

Social Pressures: Saying no to social obligations or peer pressure to spend can prevent you from indulging in activities that strain your budget. It's important to set boundaries and be honest with yourself and others about what you can afford. Politely declining invitations or suggesting more budget-friendly alternatives can help you stay on track with your saving goals.

Unwanted Subscriptions or Services: Many individuals accumulate subscriptions or services that they no longer use or need. By learning to say no to renewing or signing up for unnecessary subscriptions, such as streaming services, gym memberships, or magazine subscriptions, you can save a significant amount of money over time.

Loans and Borrowing: Saying no to excessive borrowing or lending money can help you avoid unnecessary interest charges, fees, or potential strains on relationships. Prioritizing financial stability over impulsive borrowing can lead to better long-term savings and reduce financial stress.

Time and Energy: Learning to say no to commitments, tasks, or projects that don't align with your priorities or values can help you save valuable time and energy. By focusing on activities that truly matter to you, you can use your resources more efficiently and effectively.

Remember, saying no doesn't mean you have to isolate yourself or be selfish. It's about setting healthy boundaries, making conscious choices, and prioritizing your financial well-being.

Example:

Here's an example to illustrate how learning to say no can help you save:

Let's say your friends invite you to go on a weekend trip to a popular tourist destination. While it sounds like a fun opportunity, you realize that the trip would be quite expensive and doesn't align with your current saving goals. Instead of impulsively saying yes and compromising your budget, you decide to say no and explain your financial situation.

By saying no to the expensive trip, you save on transportation costs, accommodation expenses, dining out, and various other travel-related expenses. You can then redirect that money towards your savings, whether it's for an emergency fund, paying off debts, or saving for a specific goal, such as a down payment on a house or a dream vacation in the future.

In addition, by saying no, you also avoid potential stress associated with overspending or accumulating debt. You maintain control over your finances and prioritize your long-term financial well-being.

Remember, it's important to communicate your decision respectfully and honestly to your friends. You can suggest alternative, more affordable ways to spend time together, such as organizing a local outing or having a gathering at someone's home. This way, you can still enjoy social activities while staying within your budget and continuing to save.

Record your expenses

Before you plan your savings, first put down all your expenses to know how much you spend on things. Make sure you include everything you could remember on your list of expenses from small things like pens to big one like house rent.

Even after you have started saving, still keep track of your expenses to know where your money is really going. Records like this will make it easy for you to derive a good budgeting and saving strategies that will suit your lifestyle.

How recording your expenses can make you save till you get rich and beyond

Recording your expenses can be a powerful tool to help you save money in several ways:

Increased Awareness: When you record your expenses, you become more aware of where your money is going. It allows you to see the big picture of your spending habits and identify areas where you may be overspending or making unnecessary purchases. This awareness can motivate you to make better financial decisions and cut back on non-essential expenses.

Budgeting: By keeping track of your expenses, you can create a budget based on your income and financial goals. Having a budget helps you allocate your money wisely, ensuring that you prioritize savings and essential expenses before discretionary spending. It allows you to set limits for each category and track your progress towards your savings goals.

Identifying Patterns: When you record your expenses consistently over time, you can identify patterns and trends in your spending behavior. For example, you may notice that you spend a significant amount of money on dining out or impulse purchases. Recognizing these patterns enables you to make targeted changes and find ways to reduce or eliminate unnecessary expenses.

Accountability and Discipline: Recording your expenses creates a sense of accountability. You become more mindful of your spending choices because you know you have to track and record them. This increased discipline can help you resist impulse purchases, evaluate the true value of each expense, and make more deliberate financial decisions.

Goal Setting and Progress Tracking: Tracking your expenses allows you to set specific financial goals, such as saving for a vacation, paying off debt, or building an emergency fund. By regularly recording your expenses, you can monitor your progress towards these goals and make adjustments if necessary. Seeing your savings grow over time can provide a sense of accomplishment and motivate you to continue saving.

Decision Making: When you have a clear record of your expenses, you can make informed decisions about your spending. For example, you can compare prices, evaluate the value of different products or services, and determine if certain expenses align with your priorities. This can help you make smarter purchasing choices and avoid unnecessary expenses.

Overall, recording your expenses helps you develop better financial habits, become more mindful of your spending, and make conscious choices that prioritize saving. By understanding where your money goes and making adjustments based on that knowledge, you can increase your savings and work towards achieving your financial goals.

Example:

Let's take a practical example to illustrate how recording your expenses can help you save money:

Let's say you start recording your expenses for a month, and you notice that you spend a significant amount of money on eating out at restaurants. By tracking your expenses, you become aware that this is a major area where you can make adjustments to save money.

Based on this information, you decide to set a budget for dining out and allocate a specific amount of money each month for this category. This budget allows you to enjoy eating out occasionally while still being conscious of your spending.

As you continue to record your expenses, you notice that you often make impulsive purchases on clothing and accessories. This realization prompts you to reevaluate your spending habits and make a conscious effort to resist unnecessary purchases.

Additionally, by tracking your expenses, you notice that you're spending a significant amount of money on subscription services that you rarely use. Armed with this knowledge, you can cancel or downgrade those subscriptions, freeing up more money to put towards savings.

Over time, as you consistently record your expenses and make adjustments based on the insights gained, you start to see positive changes in your saving habits. You are more mindful of your spending choices, prioritize essential expenses and savings, and cut back on non-essential purchases. As a result, you begin to accumulate more savings and make progress towards your financial goals.

By using the recorded expenses as a guide, you can make informed decisions about your spending, identify areas where you can save, and stay on track with your budget. Ultimately, this disciplined approach to recording and analyzing your expenses helps you become more intentional with your money and achieve greater financial stability.

The Golden Ratio

This is a basic Budgeting hack where one needs to break costs into the monetary course of events of the present, past, and future. Fundamentally, it is the breaking down of your monthly spending by working out the amount of your gross pay that has gone into your past bills, how much is going into your current bills, and how much will go into future reserve funds.

By taking proper review of your past record of expenditure, you will comprehend the amount of your pay you ought to dispense to your current spending, and future reserve funds. It may be 20% for past bills, 60% for current expenses, and 20 percent for future reserve funds, so the ratio can be 20:60:20. That is called The Golden Ratio (20:60:20): 20% for past bills, 60% for current expenses, and 20 percent for future savings. This proportion can be adjusted according to individual needs.

The golden ratio budget repeats the more commonly used 50-30-20 budget that suggests using half of your pay on need, 30% on wants and 20% on future savings. The "needs" category covers housing, food, utilities, protection, transportation and other important expenses of living.

Which is the best proportion for planning?

One of the most well-known sorts of rate based financial plans is the 50/30/20 rule that I have highlighted as hack no 2. The thought is to partition your pay into three classifications, burning through half on needs, 30% on wants, and 20% on reserve or future funds.

However, what works for Peter might not work for Paul. So the golden ratio might be the best budgeting ratio for you.

How using the golden ratio can make you save till you get rich and beyond

The golden ratio is a mathematical concept often associated with aesthetics and design. While it may not have a direct impact on saving money, you can apply principles inspired by the golden ratio to develop habits and strategies that promote saving. Here are a few ways you can use the golden ratio to enhance your savings:

Budget Allocation: The golden ratio suggests a division into two parts, where the ratio of the larger part to the smaller part is the same as the ratio of the whole to the larger part. You can apply this principle to budgeting by allocating your income in a similar way. For example, you can aim to spend 60% of your income on necessities and save the remaining 40%. This balanced approach helps prioritize saving while maintaining a reasonable standard of living.

Proportional Saving: Another approach is to save a certain proportion of any windfall or additional income you receive. For instance, if you receive a bonus, an inheritance, or a raise, you can save a fixed percentage (e.g., 1.618, which is an approximation of the golden ratio) and allocate the rest for other purposes.

Expense Evaluation: The golden ratio can also be applied to evaluating your expenses. Analyze your spending patterns and identify areas where you may be overspending or allocating an excessive portion of your budget. By aiming to align your expenses with a more balanced ratio, you can trim unnecessary spending and redirect those funds towards savings.

Investment Diversification: Diversifying your investments is a prudent financial strategy. Applying the golden ratio concept, you can allocate your investment portfolio across different asset classes in a balanced way. This ensures that your savings are not overly concentrated in a single investment, reducing the risk of significant losses.

Long-Term Planning: The golden ratio can also guide your long-term savings goals. Divide your desired target amount into two parts, with the larger part representing the goal itself and the smaller part serving as a milestone or interim target. This approach allows you to celebrate smaller achievements along the way, motivating you to continue saving until you reach the ultimate goal.

Remember, while the golden ratio can provide some inspiration and structure, it's essential to adapt these principles to your specific financial circumstances and goals. Developing good saving habits, creating a budget, and seeking professional financial advice when necessary are all crucial steps in building a strong foundation for savings.

Example:

Here's an example to illustrate how you can apply the golden ratio to your savings:

Let's say your monthly income is $3,000. Using the golden ratio approach, you can allocate your income as follows:

Necessities: Allocate 60% of your income for necessities such as rent, utilities, groceries, transportation, and other essential expenses. In this case, 60% of $3,000 is $1,800.

Savings: Allocate the remaining 40% of your income towards savings. In this case, 40% of $3,000 is $1,200.

By following this allocation, you prioritize your savings while ensuring that a significant portion of your income covers your essential needs. It strikes a balance between responsible spending and saving for the future.

Now, let's consider a scenario where you receive a bonus of $1,000. Applying the proportional saving concept inspired by the golden ratio, you can save a certain proportion of this windfall. For instance:

Save 61.8% (approximation of the golden ratio) of the bonus amount: 61.8% of $1,000 is $618.

Allocate the remaining 38.2% for other purposes: 38.2% of $1,000 is $382.

By saving a portion of your bonus, you continue to reinforce your savings habits and make progress towards your financial goals.

These examples demonstrate how you can use the golden ratio as a guiding principle to allocate your income, handle windfalls, and maintain a balanced approach to saving. Remember, personal finance is highly individual, so feel free to adapt these percentages based on your own circumstances and priorities.

Cut your spending

Another thing that will help you to save is to cut your spending. Look deeply on your lifestyles and cut spending on things that are not as important as you might think. You might still be doing them if they are not avoidable but the term is to 'cut' your spending on them since they are not so important to your existence. It is each person that will determine nonessentials because what you consider as non essentials might be essentials for others but just don't deceive yourself.

How cutting your spending can make you save till you get rich and beyond

Cutting your spending can be an effective way to save money because it allows you to reduce unnecessary expenses and allocate your resources more efficiently. Here are several ways in which cutting spending can help you save:

Identify and eliminate non-essential expenses: Review your monthly budget and identify areas where you can reduce or eliminate non-essential expenses. This could include dining out less frequently, canceling unused subscriptions or memberships, or cutting back on entertainment expenses.

Create a budget and track your spending: Establishing a budget helps you gain better control over your finances. Determine your income and allocate specific amounts for different categories of expenses, such as housing, transportation, groceries, and entertainment. By tracking your spending, you can identify areas where you're overspending and make adjustments accordingly.

Differentiate between needs and wants: Differentiating between essential needs and discretionary wants is crucial for cutting spending. Prioritize your needs, such as food, housing, utilities, and transportation, over non-essential wants. By reducing discretionary spending on things like luxury items or impulse purchases, you can save more money.

Comparison shopping and negotiating: When making purchases, compare prices from different vendors or stores to ensure you're getting the best deal. Take advantage of sales, discounts, or promotional offers. Additionally, negotiate for lower prices when possible, such as when purchasing a car or negotiating your cable or internet bill.

Minimize recurring expenses: Review your monthly bills and identify recurring expenses that can be minimized or eliminated. For example, consider reducing your cable package, finding a more affordable cell phone plan, or exploring options to lower your utility bills through energy-saving practices.

Reduce dining out and cook at home: Dining out frequently can quickly add up. By cooking meals at home, you can save a significant amount of money. Plan your meals, create shopping lists, and buy groceries in bulk to further optimize your savings.

Save on transportation costs: Transportation expenses, such as fuel, maintenance, and public transportation fees, can be significant. Explore alternatives like carpooling, using public transportation, biking, or walking when feasible. These options not only reduce expenses but also have environmental benefits.

Avoid unnecessary debt: High-interest debt, such as credit card debt, can consume a substantial portion of your income. Minimize your reliance on credit cards and strive to pay off existing debt as quickly as possible. This way, you can save on interest charges and have more funds available for saving.

Prioritize quality over quantity: When making purchases, consider the long-term value and quality of an item rather than solely focusing on the price tag. Investing in durable, high-quality products can save you money in the long run, as they typically last longer and require fewer replacements.

Set savings goals: Finally, establish clear savings goals to motivate yourself. Whether it's saving for a down payment on a house, an emergency fund, or a vacation, having specific targets in mind can help you stay disciplined and committed to cutting spending.

Remember, saving money requires discipline and consistent effort. By cutting your spending in various areas of your life, you can significantly increase your savings over time and improve your overall financial well-being.

Example:

Here's an example to illustrate how cutting your spending can lead to saving money:

Let's say you have identified that you spend an average of $200 per month on eating out at restaurants. By cutting back on dining out and cooking more meals at home, you estimate that you can reduce your restaurant expenses by 50%.

Initial monthly spending on dining out: $200

After cutting back by 50%: $100

Monthly savings: $200 − $100 = $100

By making this change, you can save $100 per month, which amounts to $1,200 per year. This saved money can be allocated towards other financial goals, such as building an emergency fund, paying off debt, or investing for the future.

Remember that this is just one example, and the actual impact on your savings will depend on your specific circumstances and spending habits. It's important to review your own expenses and identify areas where you can cut back to achieve your desired savings goals.

Set goals for saving

Setting goals for saving is the fuel that will keep you going even when things are tough. Think about how much you want to save, what you need the savings for, when you want to achieve all or one of your saving goals.

Your saving goals must comprise short, medium and long term goals. Then estimate how much money you'll need for each goal and how long it might take you to save it.

Also try to make your life fun through your savings by setting a small achievable short-term goal for something useful and fancy such as a new laptop or phone. Try to save and buy things for yourself. Also save to buy gifts for people. Don't let your savings make you stingy. If you help people with your money, people will help you too with their money though might not come from the people you help directly.

Buying things for yourself and others will make your savings meaningful, helpful and will inspire you to save more.

How setting goals for saving can help you save till you get rich and beyond

Setting goals for saving is an essential step in the journey towards building wealth. By establishing clear and specific financial objectives, you create a roadmap that guides your actions and keeps you motivated. Here's how setting goals for saving can help you save until you become financially prosperous:

Clarity and focus: Setting financial goals provides clarity about what you want to achieve. It helps you identify the amount of money you need to accumulate and the timeframe within which you want to achieve it. This focus enables you to make informed decisions and prioritize your saving efforts.

Motivation and discipline: Goals act as powerful motivators. When you have a specific target in mind, such as saving a certain amount of money or reaching a particular net worth, you are more likely to stay disciplined and committed to your saving plan. Goals serve as reminders of the larger purpose behind your saving efforts.

Tracking progress: Setting goals allows you to track your progress over time. You can measure your achievements and see how far you've come. This tracking process helps you stay accountable and make adjustments if needed. Celebrating milestones along the way can also boost your motivation and reinforce positive saving habits.

Breaking it down: Big financial goals can often feel overwhelming. Setting smaller, manageable milestones or short-term objectives that align with your long-term goal can make the process more attainable. Breaking down the larger goal into smaller, actionable steps enables you to take consistent actions towards your ultimate objective.

Budgeting and planning: Goals provide a framework for budgeting and planning your finances effectively. When you have a clear target in mind, you can evaluate your income, expenses, and savings rate to ensure you're on track to reach your goal. This process allows you to allocate resources more efficiently and make informed decisions about spending and saving.

Adjusting strategies: As you progress towards your goal, you may encounter unforeseen circumstances or changes in your financial situation. By regularly reviewing your goals, you can adapt your saving strategies accordingly. Adjustments may include increasing or decreasing your savings rate, exploring new investment opportunities, or reevaluating your timeframes.

Building good financial habits: Setting and working towards goals instills discipline and develops good financial habits. By consistently saving a portion of your income, you establish a pattern of responsible financial behavior. These habits, when maintained over time, can help you accumulate wealth and maintain financial stability in the long run.

Remember, setting goals for saving is just the first step. It's crucial to develop a comprehensive financial plan, educate yourself about investing, and remain committed to your objectives. Building wealth is a long-term endeavor that requires patience, persistence, and adaptability.

Example:

Here's an example of how setting goals for saving can help you save until you become financially prosperous:

Goal: Save $100,000 for a down payment on a house within five years.

Clarity and focus: By setting this specific goal, you have a clear target in mind, which is to accumulate $100,000 for a down payment. This clarity allows you to make informed decisions and prioritize your saving efforts towards this objective.

Motivation and discipline: The goal of owning a home can be a powerful motivator. It keeps you disciplined and committed to your saving plan, as you understand that reaching this goal will bring you closer to your vision of financial prosperity and stability.

Tracking progress: Over the course of five years, you can track your progress towards saving $100,000. Each month or quarter, you can evaluate how much you've saved and adjust your saving strategies accordingly. Seeing the incremental progress can keep you motivated and engaged in the saving process.

Breaking it down: To achieve this goal, you can break it down into smaller milestones. For example, you can aim to save $20,000 each year or approximately $1,667 per month. This smaller target makes the goal more manageable and allows you to focus on achievable steps along the way.

Budgeting and planning: With a specific savings goal, you can create a budget and allocate your income accordingly. You can analyze your expenses, identify areas where you can reduce spending, and direct those savings towards your down payment fund. This budgeting process helps you stay on track and ensures you're making progress towards your goal.

Adjusting strategies: As time goes by, you may encounter changes in your financial situation or unexpected expenses. By regularly reviewing your goal, you can adapt your saving strategies if necessary. For instance, if you receive a raise or a bonus, you can consider increasing your monthly savings amount to accelerate your progress.

Building good financial habits: Throughout the five-year period, you'll develop good financial habits such as consistently saving a portion of your income, tracking your expenses, and making intentional financial decisions. These habits will continue to serve you well even after you achieve your savings goal, enabling you to maintain financial stability and continue building wealth.

Remember, this is just one example, and your goals will vary based on your unique circumstances and aspirations. It's important to tailor your goals to your specific financial situation and regularly review and adjust them as needed.

Prioritize your finances

To achieve a meaningful lifestyle, you should be able to know your priorities and put them according to their scale of preference. Know what is more important to you after your daily expenses. For instance, if you are going to need to buy or build a house, the best thing is to start saving for it now. If you will need savings for your retirement , start the savings now and don't wait until later. The money you will be allocating might be small but it means something. If saving for your children's education is a priority to you then start saving now. If you want to save for your health in case you grow old, start now. Prioritizing your savings goals can give you a clear idea of how to allocate your savings.

How prioritizing your finances can make you save till you get rich and beyond

Prioritizing your finances is an effective way to save money because it allows you to allocate your resources wisely and focus on your financial goals. Here are some key steps to help you prioritize your finances and boost your savings:

Create a budget: Start by understanding your income and expenses. Make a detailed budget that outlines all your sources of income and tracks your expenses. This will give you a clear picture of where your money is going and help you identify areas where you can cut back.

Set financial goals: Define your short-term and long-term financial goals. These could include saving for emergencies, paying off debt, buying a house, or investing for retirement. Having specific goals helps you stay motivated and gives you a clear purpose for saving.

Differentiate between needs and wants: Distinguish between essential expenses (needs) and discretionary spending (wants). Prioritize your needs and allocate a portion of your income towards them. By reducing unnecessary expenses, you'll have more money available to save.

Build an emergency fund: Creating an emergency fund is a crucial step in prioritizing your finances. Aim to save three to six months' worth of living expenses in a separate account. This fund acts as a safety net in case of unexpected events, such as job loss or medical emergencies.

Pay off high-interest debt: Prioritize paying off high-interest debt, such as credit card balances, as quickly as possible. The interest charges on these debts can accumulate rapidly, so allocating extra funds towards paying them off will save you money in the long run.

Automate your savings: Set up automatic transfers from your checking account to a separate savings account. By automating your savings, you'll ensure a consistent contribution towards your goals without the temptation to spend the money elsewhere.

Cut unnecessary expenses: Review your budget and identify areas where you can reduce or eliminate expenses. This could include dining out less frequently, canceling unused subscriptions, negotiating better deals on utilities, or finding cost-effective alternatives for your everyday needs.

Track your progress: Regularly monitor your financial progress. Keep an eye on your savings, track your spending, and evaluate your budget to ensure you're on track to meet your goals. Adjust your priorities if necessary and celebrate milestones along the way to stay motivated.

Seek professional advice: If you're unsure about financial planning or need assistance with complex matters like investments or retirement planning, consider consulting with a financial advisor. They can provide personalized advice based on your circumstances and help you make informed decisions.

Remember, the key to successful financial prioritization is discipline and consistency. By aligning your spending habits with your financial goals, you can make significant progress in saving money and securing your financial future.

Example:

Here's an example to illustrate how prioritizing your finances can lead to savings:

Let's say you have a monthly income of $3,000 and you want to save money for an emergency fund, pay off your credit card debt, and save for a vacation.

Create a budget:

Fixed expenses (needs):

Rent/mortgage: $1,000
Utilities: $200
Groceries: $300
Transportation: $200
Insurance: $100

Total fixed expenses: $1,800
Variable expenses (wants):

Dining out/entertainment: $200
Shopping: $100
Total variable expenses: $300
Savings and debt repayment goals:

Emergency fund: $500
Credit card debt repayment: $300
Vacation savings: $200
Total budgeted expenses: $2,800

Prioritize your goals:

Allocate $500 towards building your emergency fund to reach your target of $6,000 within a year.
Allocate $300 towards paying off your high-interest credit card debt.
Allocate $200 towards saving for your vacation.
Adjust your spending habits:

Reduce dining out/entertainment expenses to $100, saving $100.
Cut back on shopping expenses to $50, saving $50.
Automate savings and debt repayment:

Set up an automatic transfer of $500 to your emergency fund each month.

Set up an automatic payment of $300 towards your credit card debt.

By prioritizing your finances in this example, you've managed to allocate your income towards your goals effectively. You're saving $500 each month for your emergency fund, making consistent progress on paying off your credit card debt with $300 per month, and setting aside $200 each month for your vacation.

Additionally, by cutting back on unnecessary expenses like dining out and shopping, you're saving an extra $150 per month. Over time, these adjustments and consistent savings will accumulate, allowing you to reach your financial goals faster and build a healthy savings habit.

Remember, this is just a simplified example, and everyone's financial situation is unique. Adjust the numbers and goals to align with your own circumstances and priorities.

Choose the right accounts

Another working strategy that could help you to save money is by having or chosen one or more savings and investment accounts for short- and long-term goals taking into consideration factors like minimum amount to open the account, minimum balance in the account charges, interest rates, risk and how soon you'll need the money.

Several savings and investment accounts available for U.S residents include FDIC-insured deposit account which is good for short term savings, Certificate of Deposit (CD), which is good for medium term savings since it locks in your money for a fixed period of time at a rate that is typically higher than that of a savings account and FDIC-insured individual retirement accounts (IRAs) or 529 plans, which are tax-efficient savings accounts as well as securities, such as stocks or mutual funds for long-term goals like saving for retirement or your child's education.

How choosing the right accounts can make you save till you get rich and beyond

Choosing the right accounts can play a significant role in helping you save money and work towards building wealth. Here are some key considerations:

High-Interest Savings Account: Look for a savings account that offers a competitive interest rate. This allows your money to grow over time, helping you save more effectively.

Tax-Advantaged Retirement Accounts: Contributing to retirement accounts like 401(k)s, IRAs, or similar options can offer tax advantages and potential employer matches. These accounts provide a long-term savings strategy, helping you build wealth for retirement while reducing your taxable income.

Investment Accounts: Consider opening an investment account, such as a brokerage account, to invest in stocks, bonds, mutual funds, or exchange-traded funds (ETFs). Investing wisely can potentially yield higher returns over time, accelerating your wealth-building efforts.

Cashback or Rewards Credit Cards: Choosing credit cards that offer cashback or rewards can help you earn benefits on your everyday spending. Be sure to use them responsibly by paying off the balance in full each month to avoid interest charges.

Debt Consolidation: If you have multiple high-interest debts, such as credit cards or personal loans, consider consolidating them into a lower-interest loan. This can reduce the overall interest you pay and help you save money in the long run.

High-Yield Certificates of Deposit (CDs): CDs offer fixed interest rates over a specific period, making them a low-risk option for saving. Look for institutions offering higher rates to maximize your returns.

Automatic Savings Transfers: Set up automatic transfers from your checking account to your savings or investment accounts. This way, you can ensure consistent savings without relying on your willpower alone.

Fee-Free or Low-Fee Accounts: Pay attention to account fees, such as monthly maintenance fees or transaction fees. Look for accounts that offer fee-free services or accounts with low fees to minimize unnecessary expenses.

Emergency Fund: Maintaining an emergency fund in a separate savings account can help you cover unexpected expenses without derailing your long-term financial goals. Aim to save three to six months' worth of living expenses in this fund.

Regular Monitoring and Adjustments: Continuously review your accounts, assess their performance, and make necessary adjustments. Consider consulting with a financial advisor to optimize your savings and investment strategies.

Remember, while choosing the right accounts is essential, it's equally important to have a disciplined approach to saving and spending. Developing good financial habits, such as budgeting, avoiding unnecessary debt, and living within your means, will contribute to your overall financial success.

Example:

Let's consider an example to illustrate how choosing the right accounts can help you save and potentially grow your wealth.

Let's say you have a goal to save $10,000 over the next five years. Here's how selecting the right accounts can make a difference:

High-Interest Savings Account: You open a high-interest savings account with an annual interest rate of 2%. By regularly depositing a portion of your income into this account, you can earn interest on your savings, helping your money grow over time.

Retirement Account: If your employer offers a 401(k) with a matching contribution, you contribute a percentage of your salary, and your employer matches that contribution up to a certain limit. This not only helps you save for retirement but also provides an immediate boost to your savings through the employer match.

Investment Account: You open a brokerage account and invest a portion of your savings in a diversified portfolio of stocks and bonds. Over time, the potential returns from these investments can help your wealth grow, especially if you take a long-term approach.

Cashback Credit Card: You use a cashback credit card for your everyday purchases, paying off the balance in full each month. By earning cashback rewards, you effectively save money on your regular expenses.

Debt Consolidation: Suppose you have credit card debt with high-interest rates. You consolidate your debt into a personal loan with a lower interest rate, reducing the overall interest you pay and freeing up more money for savings.

Emergency Fund: You maintain a separate high-yield savings account for your emergency fund. By consistently contributing to this account, you build a safety net that protects you from unexpected expenses without disrupting your long-term savings goals.

By combining these strategies and making smart financial choices, you increase the likelihood of reaching your savings goal of $10,000 within the set timeframe. Additionally, as you continue to save and invest wisely, your wealth can grow over the long term, helping you work towards achieving financial independence and potentially building greater wealth.

Auto save your money

Another thing that will help in achieving your saving goals is to have a separate account for savings and make sure you are transferring money from payment made into your main account to that particular savings account automatically. You can make this arrangement with your bank. You can also be transferring money automatically from your salary account to your savings account. Don't wait till you will be doing this yourself because you might be feeling reluctant most times because of piling expenses. You can also have an investment account where you transfer part of your money either from check, salary or even saving account. This will help you to meet up with your investment goals overtime.

How auto saving your money can make you save till you get rich and beyond

Auto-saving money can be a powerful tool to help you save consistently and eventually accumulate wealth. Here's how it can contribute to your journey towards becoming rich:

Consistency: Auto-saving ensures that a fixed amount of money is automatically transferred from your income to your savings on a regular basis. By automating this process, you eliminate the risk of forgetting or skipping a savings contribution. Consistency is key when it comes to building wealth because it allows your savings to grow steadily over time.

Forced Discipline: Auto-saving imposes discipline on your spending habits. Since the savings are automatically deducted before you have access to the money, it reduces the temptation to spend it impulsively. This method helps you develop a savings routine and encourages financial discipline.

Prioritizing Savings: By setting up automatic transfers to your savings account, you establish the habit of paying yourself first. Rather than spending all your income and saving whatever is left, auto-saving ensures that saving becomes a priority. This mindset shift can be instrumental in accumulating wealth over time.

Accumulating Compound Interest: When you consistently save money, it can be invested to earn compound interest. Compound interest allows your savings to grow exponentially as both your principal and interest earn further interest. By starting early and allowing your savings to compound over time, you can significantly increase your wealth.

Long-Term Planning: Auto-saving encourages long-term planning and goal setting. By automating your savings, you can allocate funds towards specific financial goals such as retirement, purchasing a house, starting a business, or investing in assets. This systematic approach helps you make progress towards your objectives and builds wealth over time.

Reduced Financial Stress: Knowing that you are consistently saving and working towards your financial goals can reduce stress and provide peace of mind. Auto-saving helps you establish a financial safety net and prepares you for unexpected expenses or emergencies. This, in turn, allows you to focus on other aspects of your life and career without constant worry about your financial situation.

Remember that auto-saving alone is not enough to guarantee wealth accumulation. It should be coupled with smart financial planning, budgeting, and investment strategies. Continuously educating yourself about personal finance, seeking professional advice, and staying committed to your savings goals are essential for long-term financial success.

Example:

Let's say you set up an auto-saving plan where $200 is automatically transferred from your paycheck to your savings account every month. Here's how it can help you accumulate wealth over time:

Consistency: Every month, without fail, $200 is saved automatically. Over the course of a year, you will have saved $2,400. This consistent savings habit continues year after year, allowing your savings to grow steadily.

Forced Discipline: With auto-saving, the $200 is deducted before you even see it in your checking account. This helps curb impulsive spending and forces you to live within your means. By avoiding unnecessary expenses, you are able to allocate more funds towards saving and wealth accumulation.

Accumulating Compound Interest: Let's assume your savings account earns an annual interest rate of 3%. As you continue to save and maintain a balance, your savings will start earning compound interest. Over time, the interest earned on your savings will grow, accelerating the rate of wealth accumulation.

Long-Term Planning: As your savings continue to grow, you can allocate them towards long-term goals. For instance, you might invest a portion of your savings in stocks, bonds, or real estate to further increase your wealth. Auto-saving allows you to consistently contribute towards these investments and work towards achieving your financial objectives.

Increased Savings Over Time: As your income grows or as you find opportunities to cut expenses, you can increase the amount of money you auto-save. For example, if you manage to increase your monthly auto-saving amount to $300 after a few years, your savings will grow at an accelerated rate.

Benefit of Time: By starting early and consistently auto-saving, you give your money more time to grow. Over several years or decades, the power of compounding can have a significant impact on your wealth. The longer you save, the more your money can work for you.

Remember, this is just a simplified example, and actual results may vary based on factors such as interest rates, investment returns, and individual financial situations. It's important to assess your specific circumstances, set realistic savings goals, and make informed financial decisions.

Monitor the growth of your savings

Make sure you are monitoring the progress of your savings every month. This will help you to see loopholes in your saving patterns as well as things that are making it hard for you to meet up with your plan. Monitoring your savings pattern every month will also help you to stick to your plan or want to do better the next month. It can also let you see if you will need to adjust some things like expenses for better results. Improving your savings will be a source of inspiration for you to do better in the following months.

How monitoring the growth of your savings can make you save till you get rich till you and beyond

Monitoring the growth of your savings is an essential practice that can help you save and work towards building wealth. Here's how it can contribute to your journey towards financial success:

Awareness of Progress: By regularly monitoring the growth of your savings, you gain a clear understanding of how your wealth is growing over time. This awareness can serve as a motivating factor, as you can see the positive impact of your saving efforts. It reinforces the importance of continuing to save and stay on track with your financial goals.

Tracking Performance: Monitoring the growth of your savings allows you to evaluate the performance of your investments or savings vehicles. For example, if you have invested in stocks, bonds, or mutual funds, you can track their returns and assess whether they are meeting your expectations. If certain investments consistently underperform, you may consider reevaluating your investment strategy and making necessary adjustments.

Adjusting Saving Strategies: Regular monitoring of your savings growth enables you to assess whether your saving strategies are effective or need modification. If you notice that your savings are not growing as expected, you can analyze your spending habits, identify areas where you can cut back, and allocate more funds towards savings. This active involvement in your financial progress helps you make informed decisions and adapt your approach as needed.

Long-Term Perspective: Saving for wealth accumulation is a long-term endeavor. Monitoring the growth of your savings reminds you to focus on the big picture and the end goal. It provides a sense of perspective that financial success is achieved through consistent efforts over time. Seeing incremental growth can reinforce your commitment to long-term saving and motivate you to continue until you reach your desired level of wealth.

Compound Growth: Regular monitoring of savings growth helps you fully appreciate the power of compound interest. As your savings generate returns, those returns can further contribute to your savings, leading to exponential growth over time. By actively monitoring this compounding effect, you become more aware of the benefits of long-term investing and saving, encouraging you to stay committed.

Financial Discipline: Monitoring your savings growth fosters discipline and accountability in your financial life. It encourages you to develop healthy saving habits, track your progress, and make necessary adjustments along the way. This discipline extends beyond monitoring alone and influences your overall financial behavior, including budgeting, spending decisions, and investment choices.

Remember, saving and accumulating wealth require consistent effort, discipline, and patience. Monitoring your savings growth is just one aspect of a comprehensive financial strategy. It is also crucial to diversify your investments, manage risk, seek professional advice if needed, and stay informed about financial trends and opportunities.

Example:

Let's walk through an example to illustrate how monitoring the growth of your savings can contribute to your journey towards wealth accumulation:

Imagine you have set a financial goal to save $100,000 within five years. You diligently save a portion of your income each month and invest it in a diversified portfolio of stocks and bonds.

After the first year, you start monitoring the growth of your savings regularly. You discover that your portfolio has generated a 10% return, resulting in a $10,000 increase in your savings. This progress motivates you to continue saving and reaffirms your commitment to your financial goal.

In the second year, you continue monitoring your savings growth and find that your portfolio has experienced a 12% return. This time, the growth translates to a $12,000 increase in your savings. You realize that not only are you making progress towards your goal, but your savings are also compounding, generating more significant returns.

By the end of the third year, your savings have grown by $15,000 due to a 15% return on your investments. This milestone inspires you to reassess your financial strategy and explore additional opportunities to further optimize your savings growth.

In the fourth year, you actively monitor your savings growth, track the performance of your investments, and adjust your strategy accordingly. With a 14% return, your savings increase by $14,000. However, during this period, you identify an underperforming investment in your portfolio. You decide to reallocate those funds to a more promising investment, which ultimately leads to improved returns.

As you enter the fifth and final year, you closely monitor the growth of your savings, anticipating the final push towards your goal. With a 16% return, your savings surge by $16,000, surpassing the $100,000 mark. You have successfully achieved your financial goal of saving $100,000, and the habit of monitoring your savings growth played a significant role in your accomplishment.

Throughout this example, monitoring the growth of your savings provided you with crucial insights, such as the progress made, the impact of compounding, and the need for adjustments in your investment strategy. It also helped you stay motivated, maintain financial discipline, and make informed decisions. By actively tracking your savings growth, you were able to save till you got rich, reaching your financial goal and building a foundation for long-term wealth.

Pay off your debt

One truth is that debt cannot make us grow, rather it is a minus to our financial worth. Therefore it is quite important to find a way to pay off our debts either before we start saving or clear it with our savings. If we pay our debts with our savings, then we can start fresh savings and it is this one that can help us save till we get rich. Debt with high interest rates should be cleared as soon as you can because not paying off the debt means you're wasting money on interest rates and can make your credit score take a hit.

Debt with high interest rates will add up quickly to a large sum over time. So, it is very crucial to clear it in time so that you can enjoy your savings. Though it is not easy to pay a large sum of debt, thinking about how the debt could quickly get out of hand can help you to make the right decision.

Sitting down and planning how you could pay off your debt either quickly or overtimes is crucial to your saving plan and success.

How paying off your debt can help you save till you get rich and beyond

Paying off your debt can indeed help you save and work towards building wealth. Here are several ways in which paying off debt can contribute to your financial well-being and help you on the path to becoming rich:

Interest savings: Debt often comes with interest charges, which can accumulate over time and increase the total amount you owe. By paying off your debts, you eliminate these interest expenses, freeing up more money to save and invest.

Improved cash flow: Debt repayments can consume a significant portion of your monthly income. As you pay off debts, you reduce your monthly financial obligations, freeing up cash flow. This extra money can be redirected towards savings and investments, accelerating your wealth-building efforts.

Reduced financial stress: Debt can be a significant source of stress and anxiety. By eliminating debt, you remove this burden and gain peace of mind. Reduced financial stress allows you to focus on your long-term financial goals and make better decisions about saving and investing.

Increased creditworthiness: Paying off debt improves your creditworthiness and credit score. A good credit score can open doors to better financial opportunities, such as lower interest rates on loans, better credit card terms, and access to higher credit limits. These advantages can save you money in the long run and help you accumulate wealth more effectively.

Ability to leverage opportunities: Being debt-free provides you with flexibility and the ability to seize opportunities as they arise. Whether it's investing in a business venture, real estate, or the stock market, having extra funds available can help you take advantage of opportunities that can accelerate your path to wealth.

Focus on long-term financial goals: Debt often distracts us from focusing on long-term financial goals. By eliminating debt, you can shift your attention towards saving and investing for the future. Whether it's retirement planning, building an emergency fund, or investing in assets with growth potential, being debt-free allows you to allocate your resources towards these wealth-building objectives.

Building positive financial habits: Paying off debt requires discipline, budgeting, and responsible financial management. As you work towards becoming debt-free, you develop valuable financial habits that can serve you well in the future. These habits, such as budgeting, saving, and avoiding unnecessary debt, contribute to long-term financial success and wealth accumulation.

Remember, becoming rich is a multifaceted process that involves various strategies beyond debt repayment. It's important to combine debt elimination with other wealth-building techniques such as saving, investing, diversifying income streams, and continuously educating yourself about personal finance and investment opportunities.

Example

Let's consider an example to illustrate how paying off debt can help you save and work towards becoming rich:

Let's say you have the following financial situation:

Total outstanding debt: $50,000
Interest rate on debt: 15%
Minimum monthly debt payment: $1,000
Now, suppose you decide to prioritize paying off this debt aggressively. You create a budget, cut back on unnecessary expenses, and allocate extra funds towards debt repayment.

Interest savings: By aggressively paying off your debt, you can significantly reduce the interest charges. Let's assume it takes you three years to pay off the entire $50,000 debt. By doing so, you would save approximately $11,822 in interest expenses.

Improved cash flow: As you pay down your debt, your monthly financial obligations decrease. In our example, the minimum monthly debt payment is $1,000. Once you become debt-free, you will have an extra $1,000 per month available for savings and investments.

Reduced financial stress: As you make progress towards paying off your debt, you experience a sense of relief and reduced financial stress. This allows you to focus on long-term financial goals and make better decisions regarding saving and investing.

Increased creditworthiness: Successfully paying off your debt improves your creditworthiness and credit score. This improved credit score can help you secure better terms on future loans, such as lower interest rates on mortgages or business loans.

Ability to leverage opportunities: Being debt-free provides you with flexibility and the ability to seize opportunities. Let's say an investment opportunity arises that requires an initial investment of $20,000. Since you no longer have debt payments, you can redirect the extra $1,000 per month you were previously using for debt repayment towards this investment. Over time, this investment could generate substantial returns and contribute to your wealth accumulation.

Focus on long-term financial goals: With your debt paid off, you can now focus on saving and investing for the future. You can allocate the extra $1,000 per month towards building an emergency fund, contributing to retirement accounts, or investing in assets with growth potential.

By combining the benefits mentioned above and consistently following a disciplined approach to debt repayment and wealth-building, you can significantly improve your financial situation and work towards becoming rich over time.

Remember, the specific numbers and timeline in this example are for illustrative purposes only. The actual results will vary based on individual circumstances and the interest rates, amounts, and timelines of your own debt.

Eager and believe you can save money

I put this hack at number 20 because it is almost the most important hack when it comes to savings because how can you save if you are not interested and don't believe that you can do so.

Don't believe that it will be hard for you to save even if it is easy for others like your friends, family members and colleagues to save.

If others can save and change their life for the best then why can't you?

To achieve success in life, you have to first believe in yourself even if others don't believe in you. What you need is a good budget plan and strict adherence to your plan. You need discipline to save money but once you are consistent it becomes your second nature.

To develop the eagerness and desire to save money, think about what your saved money can help you to do or what someone you know has achieved with his/her savings. Thinking like that will help you develop a burning desire to save.

How believing you can save money can help you save till you get rich and beyond

Having a mindset that is eager and believing in your ability to save money can indeed be beneficial for your financial success. Here are some ways in which this mindset can help you save money and work towards becoming wealthy:

Motivation: When you are eager and believe in your ability to save, you are more motivated to take action and make the necessary changes in your financial habits. This motivation can drive you to be more disciplined and consistent in your saving efforts.

Goal Setting: Having a strong belief in your ability to save money allows you to set clear financial goals. By setting specific targets, such as saving a certain percentage of your income or reaching a specific savings milestone, you can work towards achieving those goals with determination and focus.

Budgeting: Believing that you can save money encourages you to create and stick to a budget. A budget helps you track your income and expenses, enabling you to identify areas where you can cut back and save more. With an eager mindset, you are more likely to follow through with your budget and resist unnecessary spending.

Frugal Mindset: Believing in your ability to save can foster a frugal mindset. This means being conscious of your spending habits, seeking out deals and discounts, and finding ways to cut costs without sacrificing your quality of life. Embracing a frugal lifestyle can significantly increase your savings over time.

Investing: When you are eager to save and believe in your financial abilities, you are more likely to explore investment opportunities. Investing your savings wisely can help your money grow over time, accelerating your path to wealth. This could involve investing in stocks, real estate, retirement accounts, or other investment vehicles that align with your goals and risk tolerance.

Persistence: Building wealth takes time and perseverance. By maintaining an eager and optimistic mindset, you can remain persistent even during challenging times or setbacks. Your belief in your ability to save will keep you focused on your long-term financial goals, enabling you to overcome obstacles and stay on track.

Remember that saving and building wealth is a gradual process that requires consistent effort and patience. It's important to combine a positive mindset with practical financial strategies to maximize your savings potential and work towards achieving your financial aspirations.

Example:

Here's an example to illustrate how an eager and believing mindset can help you save money and work towards becoming rich:

Deborah was a young professional who has a strong belief in her ability to save money and achieve financial success. She eagerly adopts a positive mindset and takes the following steps to save and grow her wealth:

Motivation: Deborah sets a clear goal of saving 30% of her monthly income to build an emergency fund and invest for her future. She believes that with discipline and determination, she can achieve this target.

Budgeting: Deborah creates a detailed budget that tracks her income and expenses. She identifies areas where she can cut back, such as dining out less frequently and reducing discretionary spending on unnecessary items.

Frugal Mindset: Deborah embraces a frugal lifestyle by seeking out discounts, using coupons, and making conscious spending choices. She focuses on quality rather than quantity and finds affordable alternatives for her needs.

Investing: Deborah educates herself about various investment options and starts investing a portion of her savings in a diversified portfolio of stocks and mutual funds. She believes that by investing wisely, her money can grow significantly over time.

Persistence: Deborah encounters some setbacks along the way, such as unexpected expenses or market fluctuations affecting her investments. However, her eager mindset and belief in her abilities keep her motivated. She stays committed to her financial goals and makes adjustments as needed.

Over time, Deborah's savings accumulate, and her investments generate returns. She consistently saves and invests a portion of her income, and her wealth gradually grows. With her positive mindset, she remains focused on her long-term financial goals, even during challenging times.

As Deborah's savings and investments increase, she starts to enjoy the benefits of her efforts. She gains financial security, achieves important milestones like purchasing a home, and eventually attains financial independence and wealth.

Remember, this is just an example, and individual experiences may vary. The key is to maintain a positive mindset, be disciplined in your saving habits, make smart financial decisions, and stay committed to your long-term goals.

Summary

Saving is a sure strategy to make it in life. Apart from seeing huge money at once like through retirement, business, inheritance and suchlike, saving is the surest way to increase your financial worth over time. To save, you to be mindful of the budgeting and saving hacks I highlighted in this book which include the following:

You should first create a budget

You can use the 50/30/20 rule of budget to achieve your saving goals.

You can also use the cash stuffing strategy also known as the envelope system of saving.

You can also use the Tandem saving and spending strategy by saving the actual amount you are spending.

You should also be using the pausing strategy which is to pause and think about your financial decisions

Be practical, logical and reasonable with your budget and savings.

Be checking your budget and saving plan routinely.

Your budget and saving plan should not be rigid but flexible and adjustable.

You should have plans for emergency spending since this will save you from undue frustration.

You should learn to say no to buying things on impromptu.

Try to be recording your expenses to avoid hidden expenses that you will ordinarily not know have significant values.

Just like the 50/30/20 budget ratio, the golden ratio budgeting strategy is another hack you can use.

Learn to cut your spending by only buying necessary things.

Set realistic and time based budget and saving goals.

Prioritizing your finances and expenses will help you spend on needs according to their scale of preference.

Study to know the right account for your saving goals such as short, medium, and long-term goals.

Try to save automatically by instantly splitting your money to different accounts as arranged with your bank.

Monitor the growth of your savings to know if you are moving forward or not.

One of the greatest saving hacks is to pay off your debt either before or after you start saving.

And one of the most important saving hacks is to be willing, eager and believing in your ability and capability to save.

Conclusion:

The concept of "Save Till You Get Rich And Beyond" highlights the importance of developing a disciplined savings habit as a key pathway to financial success. Throughout this discussion, we have explored various strategies and principles that can help individuals achieve their long-term financial goals.

The first and foremost lesson is the power of saving. By consistently setting aside a portion of our income and investing it wisely, we can accumulate wealth over time. The act of saving not only provides a financial cushion for unexpected expenses but also enables us to seize opportunities when they arise.

Furthermore, the concept of delayed gratification plays a crucial role in this approach. It requires resisting the temptation to spend impulsively and instead prioritizing long-term financial stability. By understanding that small sacrifices today can lead to significant rewards in the future, we can align our spending habits with our ultimate financial aspirations.

In addition to saving, investing wisely is another critical component of this philosophy. By educating ourselves about different investment options and seeking professional guidance when necessary, we can make informed decisions that generate long-term returns. Diversifying our investments and staying updated with market trends can help mitigate risks and maximize our potential for wealth accumulation.

It's important to note that the "Save Till You Get Rich And Beyond" mindset goes beyond mere frugality. It encourages us to adopt a comprehensive financial approach that encompasses budgeting, debt management, and developing multiple streams of income. By being mindful of our spending, paying off debts, and seeking additional avenues for earning, we can accelerate our journey towards financial prosperity.

The path to financial success is not linear, and setbacks and challenges are inevitable. However, by maintaining resilience, adaptability, and a long-term perspective, we can overcome obstacles and stay committed to our financial goals.

"Save Till You Get Rich And Beyond" serves as a reminder that financial success is achievable through disciplined saving, smart investing, and a comprehensive approach to personal finance. By implementing the principles discussed here, individuals can pave their way to a prosperous future and ultimately achieve their dreams and aspirations. Remember, every small step you take today brings you closer to the wealth and financial freedom you desire. So start saving, start investing, and embrace the journey towards a rich and fulfilling life.

www.ingramcontent.com/pod-product-compliance
Lightning Source LLC
Chambersburg PA
CBHW062324290526
45794CB00005B/1887